George Gershwin

Piano Duets

Arranged by

Mischa Portnoff

T0055440

Contents

chappell music company

SUMMERTIME

Music by GEORGE GERSHWIN
Lyrics by DuBOSE HEYWARD
Lyrics not included

SUMMERTIME

Music by GEORGE GERSHWIN
Lyrics by DuBOSE HEYWARD
Lyrics not included

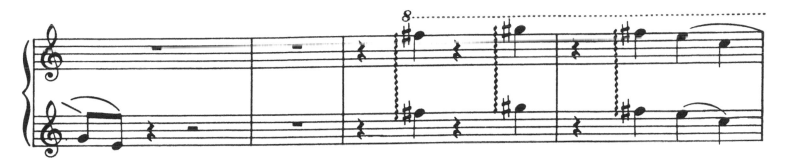

4

Secondo

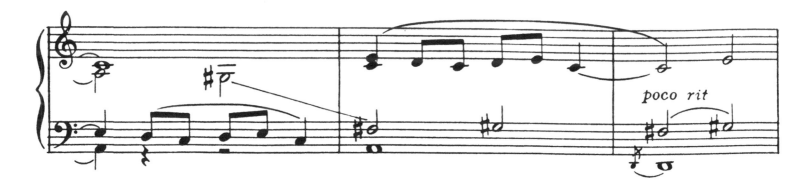

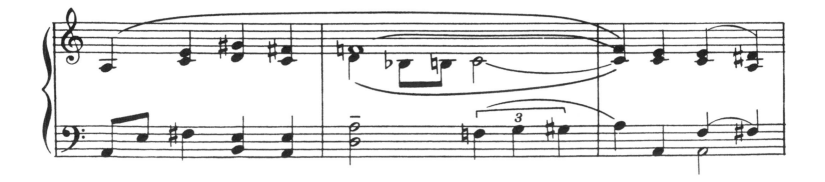

Primo

6

Secondo

Primo

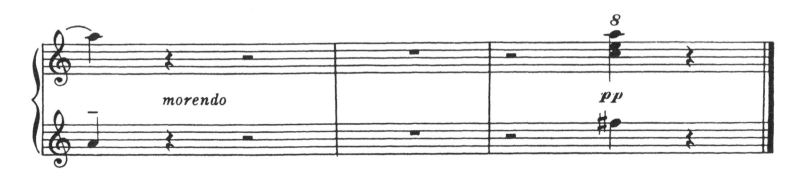

I GOT PLENTY O' NUTTIN'

Music by GEORGE GERSHWIN
Lyrics by DuBOSE HEYWARD & IRA GERSHWIN
Lyrics not included

I GOT PLENTY O' NUTTIN'

Music by GEORGE GERSHWIN
Lyrics by DuBOSE HEYWARD & IRA GERSHWIN
Lyrics not included

Secondo

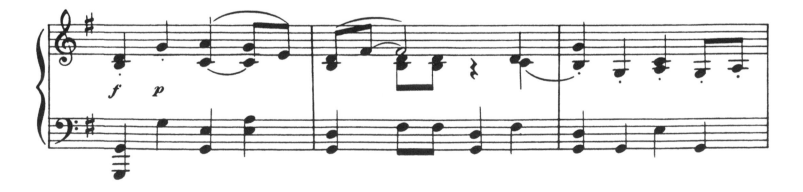

Primo

Secondo

Primo

IT AIN'T NECESSARILY SO

Music by GEORGE GERSHWIN
Lyrics by IRA GERSHWIN
Lyrics not included

IT AIN'T NECESSARILY SO

Music by GEORGE GERSHWIN
Lyrics by IRA GERSHWIN
Lyrics not included

Secondo

Primo

Secondo

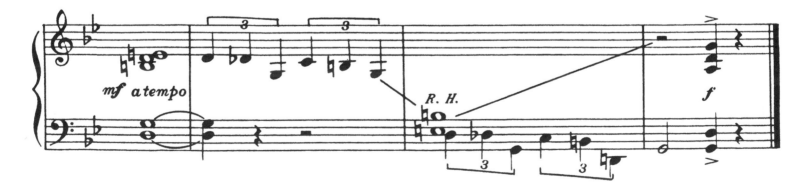

Primo

LOVE WALKED IN

Music by GEORGE GERSHWIN
Lyrics by IRA GERSHWIN
Lyrics not included

LOVE WALKED IN

Music by GEORGE GERSHWIN
Lyrics by IRA GERSHWIN
Lyrics not included

Secondo

Primo

A FOGGY DAY

Music by GEORGE GERSHWIN
Lyrics by IRA GERSHWIN
Lyrics not included

A FOGGY DAY

Music by GEORGE GERSHWIN
Lyrics by IRA GERSHWIN
Lyrics not included

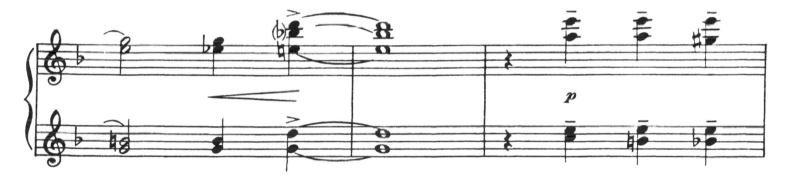

Secondo

Primo

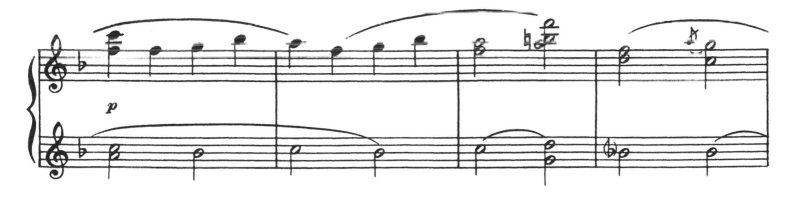

THEY CAN'T TAKE THAT AWAY FROM ME

Music by GEORGE GERSHWIN
Lyrics by IRA GERSHWIN
Lyrics not included

Slowly with warmth

Secondo

THEY CAN'T TAKE THAT AWAY FROM ME

Music by GEORGE GERSHWIN
Lyrics by IRA GERSHWIN
Lyrics not included

Secondo

Primo

LOVE IS HERE TO STAY

Music by GEORGE GERSHWIN
Lyrics by IRA GERSHWIN
Lyrics not included

Moderato

Secondo

LOVE IS HERE TO STAY

Music by GEORGE GERSHWIN
Lyrics by IRA GERSHWIN
Lyrics not included

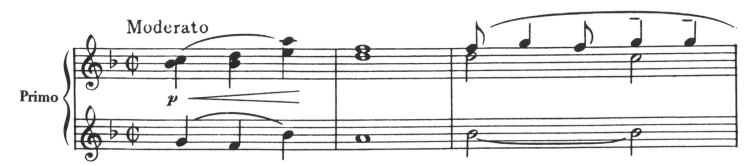

34

Secondo

Primo

I WAS DOING ALL RIGHT

Music by GEORGE GERSHWIN
Lyrics by IRA GERSHWIN
Lyrics not included

I WAS DOING ALL RIGHT

Music by GEORGE GERSHWIN
Lyrics by IRA GERSHWIN
Lyrics not included

Secondo

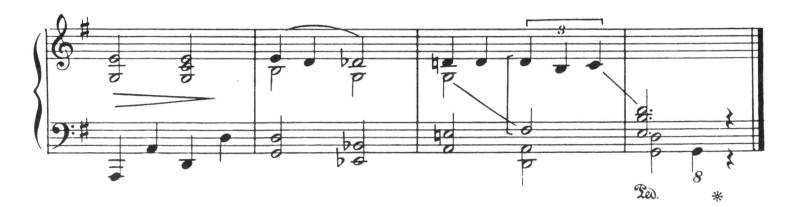

Primo

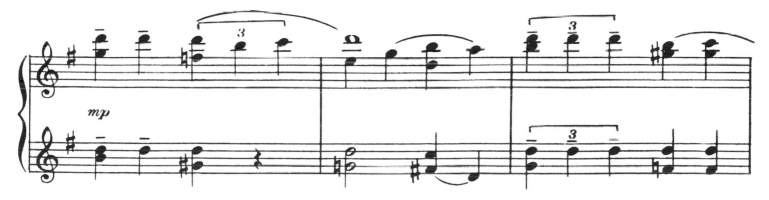

NICE WORK IF YOU CAN GET IT

Music by GEORGE GERSHWIN
Lyrics by IRA GERSHWIN
Lyrics not included

NICE WORK IF YOU CAN GET IT

Music by GEORGE GERSHWIN
Lyrics by IRA GERSHWIN
Lyrics not included

Secondo

Primo

SLAP THAT BASS

Music by GEROGE GERSHWIN
Lyrics by IRA GERSHWIN
Lyrics not included

SLAP THAT BASS

Music by GEORGE GERSHWIN
Lyrics by IRA GERSHWIN
Lyrics not included

Moderato, rhythmically

Primo

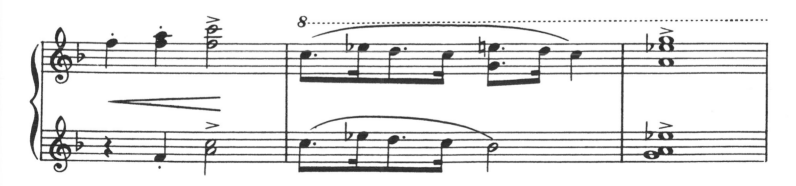

Secondo

Primo

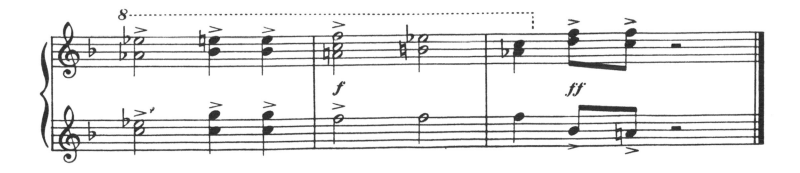